ROYAL

DREAMER

QUEEN

Save the Queen

NEVER GIVE UP

Thank you for purchasing this coloring book, one of many in the Chubby Mermaid series. Please don't forget to sign into Amzon.com – Deborah Muller Coloring Books and leave a review.

Follow me on Facebook
Chubby Mermaid Art by Deborah Muller

Join my Coloring Group on Facebook
Deborah Muller's Coloring Group

Instagram
Chubby Mermaid Art

Etsy
Chubby Mermaid

Pinterest
Deborah Muller Chubby Mermaid Art

Email
Chubbymermaid@hotmail.com

Website
ChubbyMermaidArt.com

36967256R00042

Made in the USA
Lexington, KY
19 April 2019